MW00697576

THUNDER ROLLING IN THE MOUNTAINS

by
Scott O'Dell and Ellizabeth Hall

Teacher Guide

Written by
Phyllis A. Green

Note

The Yearling paperback edition of the book published by Dell was used to prepare this guide. The page references may differ in the hardcover or other paperback editions.

Please note: Please assess the appropriateness of this book for the age level and maturity of your students prior to reading and discussing it with your class.

ISBN 978-1-56137-672-8

To order, contact your local school supply store, or—

Novel Units, Inc.
P.O. Box 97
Bulverde, TX 78163-0097

Web site: novelunits.com

Table of Contents

Skills and Strategies

Thinking
    Brainstorming, visualizing,
    evaluating, decision-making,
    synthesizing, researching

Writing
    Journaling, expository,
    titling, narrative, opinion
    pieces

Listening/Speaking
    Discussion, sounds,
    interviewing

Comprehension
    Predicting, sequencing,
    comparison/contrast

Vocabulary
    Etymology, context clues,
    prefix/suffix, word mapping

Literary Elements
    Story elements, conflict,
    similes, characterization,
    foreshadowing

Summary

Sound of Running Feet, the fourteen-year-old daughter of Chief Joseph, narrates the story of the Nez Perce tribe and the 1877 Nez Perce War. Sound of Running Feet tells of the 1,000 mile retreat of the Indians through Montana toward the Canadian border. Sound of Running Feet's own story provides a vehicle for the story, including her respect for her father, her love for Swan Necklace, and her ultimate survival.

About the Authors

Scott O'Dell worked as a technical director, cameraman, citrus rancher, teacher, and book columnist, but he spent most of his energies as a full time writer. He won many honors for his books for young people which include: *Island of the Blue Dolphins**, *The Black Pearl**, *Journey to Jericho*, *Sing Down the Moon**, *The Hawk That Dare Not Hunt by Day*, *Zia*, *Sarah Bishop**, *Streams to the River, River to the Sea: A Novel of Sacajawea**, *The Serpent Never Sleeps: A Novel of Jamestown and Pocahontas*, *Black Star, Bright Dawn*, and *My Name Is Not Angelica*.

His great-grandmother was a first cousin of the Scottish novelist Sir Walter Scott. O'Dell grew up in Julian, California, a rural gold-mining town southeast of Los Angeles, on the Mexican border in the Orifeamme Mountains. He attended Occidental College, University of Wisconsin, and Stanford.

Elizabeth Hall married O'Dell in 1967 and finished *Thunder Rolling in the Mountains* after O'Dell's death. The pair had traveled the path of Chief Joseph and the Nez Perce Indians.

*Novel Units® guides available

Overview

Thunder Rolling in the Mountains was Scott O'Dell's last book, completed after his death by his widow, Elizabeth Hall. It is a story of the Nez Perce under Chief Joseph's leadership as they sought to reach Canada while evading the U.S. military. (See Background Information, page 5 of this guide.) The reading level is listed as 5.6.

Plot summaries, vocabulary words, and discussion questions are provided chapter-by-chapter. Supplementary activities and graphics are included also. The book can be read chapter-by-chapter, predicting and thinking about what will come next. The book's interesting characters, especially Sound of Running Feet, provide opportunity to explore the writer's craft in depiction, as well as the comparisons to other fourteen-year-olds you know or have met in books. It is suggested that some instructional time be spent daily on vocabulary building. Vocabulary activities are included on page 4 of this guide. Bookmark graphics on page 7 of this guide can be used to keep track of the story and characters as it is read.

Vocabulary Activities

1. Look for nouns among the identified vocabulary words. Picture each mentally or in a simple illustration on a 3x5 card. Share your pack of pictures with a classmate. Guess the words from the illustrations. On a work paper, write down each word you guess.

2. Act out words for classmates to guess. ("Skulking," "churning," "puckered," and "commotion" are some possibilities).

3. How and when would you use each vocabulary word yourself?

4. Check out the etymology of certain vocabulary words (i.e., travois, kouse, cous, breechcloths, carbine, butte, chokeberries, gulch, papoose, nickered).

5. "Add a word a day." Distribute calendars for the time period of the novel study. Each student will meet at least one new word each day, recording it on the calendar. Evaluation is completed when the teacher chooses one of the words to be defined or used in a sentence.

6. Create a cooperative class sentence using as many vocabulary words as possible.

7. Hone the skills of using context clues. Make a class list of context clue hints. Practice "talking a word through" with a partner.

8. Keep a yearlong prefix and suffix listing—perhaps on shelf paper or adding machine tape. Review occasionally with quizzes or team competition.

9. Prepare some vocabulary games, adapting popular board games for vocabulary. At a grade level in a school, each class could author one game and prepare copies to share with other classes.

Bulletin Board Ideas

1. Use a large map to plot movements in the story.

2. Prepare a time line of the story's events.

3. Native American study: Pose questions at the start of the work. Students or groups should prepare posters to record answers and information learned.

4. Decorate blankets and tepees as the book's characters might have done.

5. Imagine you are Swan Necklace collecting colors to decorate the mats and skins your people use. Prepare your colors and sketches of what you'll paint.

Background Information

Nez Perce Indians (pronounced "nehz PURS" or "nay pehr SAY"): Nez Perce means pierced nose, a name given by a French interpreter who mistook shells worn by some of the tribe as a nose decoration. The tribe now lives in north-central Idaho, but originally lived in the region where Idaho, Oregon, and Washington meet. Prospectors overran the Nez Perce land in the 1860s when gold was found.

The Nez Perce War broke out in 1877 when government officials ordered the Nez Perce to move from their homeland in the Wallowa Valley of Oregon to a reservation in Idaho, so that white settlers could use the Wallowa Valley. Chief Joseph led a group of the Indians in their war with U.S. troops. About 70 Indians stood off about 100 soldiers in June, 1877 at White Bird Canyon, Idaho. Chief Joseph then led a band of 800 in a remarkable retreat through Montana and then north across Yellowstone Park toward the Canadian border. The Indians traveled more than 1,000 miles and surrendered at Bear Paw Mountain, 40 miles from the Canadian border. The Indians were sent to the Indian Territory in Oklahoma but were later moved to a reservation in Washington after 1885.

Initiating Activities

1. Complete a K-W-L chart. What do you know about Chief Joseph? What is the terrain of the route of the Nez Perce?

   As the book is studied, fill in this chart. Before reading, review what you KNOW (about the setting and background) in the K column. The W column is for questions you expect to have answered. The L column is completed after reading to list what you've learned.

What You Know	What You Would Like to Know	What You Learned

2. Write a journal about *surrender, leadership,* and *success*. What do these ideas mean? Try to include concrete examples from your life and reading to explain each term.

3. Do some research about the conditions for Native Americans in 1877. What do you predict for this book?

4. As a class, complete a mind map or other graphic to collect your predictions about the book. Here are some questions to aid your search for clues:

   • What does the back cover say?

   • What ideas does the picture on the cover suggest?

   • Who are the authors? What kind of books do they write?

5. Read the Foreword and look over the map in the book. What do you expect in the book?

Bookmarks to use while reading *Thunder Rolling in the Mountains*

Directions: While reading, it's always helpful to keep track of the names, places, and interesting wordings. Use these bookmarks to help.

■ *Thunder Rolling in the Mountains* ■

The Characters

■ *Thunder Rolling in the Mountains* ■

Interesting Phrases

■ *Thunder Rolling in the Mountains* ■

The Plot

Using Predictions

We all make predictions as we read—little guesses about what will happen next, how a conflict will be resolved, which details will be important to the plot, which details will help fill in our sense of a character. Students should be encouraged to predict, to make sensible guesses as they read the novel.

As students work on their predictions, these discussion questions can be used to guide them: What are some of the ways to predict? What is the process of a sophisticated reader's thinking and predicting? What clues does an author give to help us make predictions? Why are some predictions more likely to be accurate than others?

Create a chart for recording predictions. This could be either an individual or class activity. As each subsequent chapter is discussed, students can review and correct their previous predictions about plot and characters as necessary.

Use the facts and ideas the author gives.

Use your own prior knowledge.

Apply any new information (i.e., from class discussion) that may cause you to change your mind.

Predictions
_____
_____
_____
_____

Prediction Chart

What characters have we met so far?	What is the conflict in the story?	What are your predictions?	Why did you make those predictions?

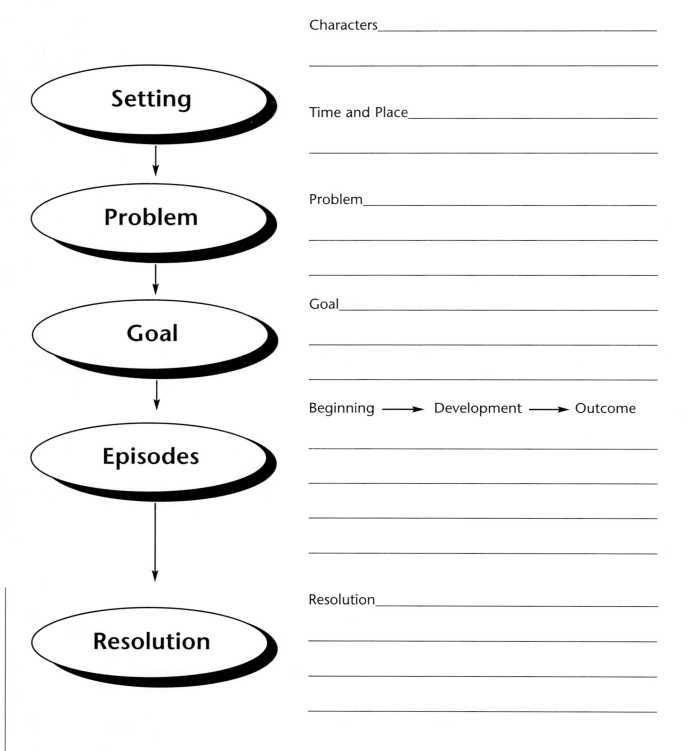

Story Map

Characters_____

_____

Time and Place_____

_____

Problem_____

_____

_____

Goal_____

_____

_____

Beginning ⟶ Development ⟶ Outcome

_____

_____

_____

_____

_____

Resolution_____

_____

_____

_____

Using Character Webs

Attribute webs are simply a visual representation of a character from the novel. They provide a systematic way for students to organize and recap the information they have about a particular character. Attribute webs may be used after reading the novel to recapitulate information about a particular character, or completed gradually as information unfolds. They may be completed individually or as a group project.

One type of character attribute web uses these divisions:

- How a character acts and feels. (How does the character act? How do you think the character feels? How would you feel if this happened to you?)

- How a character looks. (Close your eyes and picture the character. Describe him/her to me.)

- Where a character lives. (Where and when does the character live?)

- How others feel about the character. (How does another specific character feel about our character?)

In group discussion about the characters described in student attribute webs, the teacher can ask for backup proof from the novel. Inferential thinking can be included in the discussion.

Attribute webs need not be confined to characters. They may also be used to organize information about a concept, object, or place.

Attribute Web

The attribute web below will help you gather clues the author provides about a character in the novel. Fill in the blanks with words and phrases which tell how the character acts and looks, as well as what the character says and what others say about him or her.

Acts

1. _____
2. _____
3. _____
4. _____

Feels

1. _____
2. _____
3. _____
4. _____

_____

Looks

1. _____
2. _____
3. _____
4. _____

Says

1. _____
2. _____
3. _____
4. _____

Attribute Web

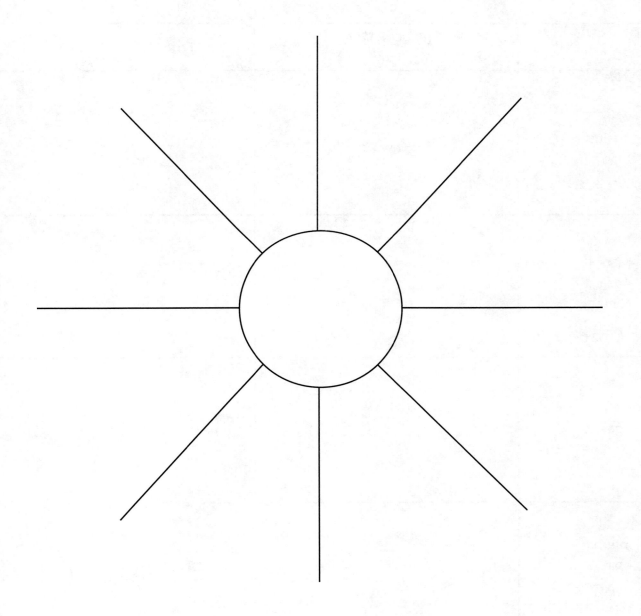

Conflicts in Literature

Background and Directions: The plots in literature are driven by conflicts and, thereby, the action in the book. Conflict can be internal to a character (What shall I do? How can I deal with my problem?) or external (dealing with outside forces like other people or natural phenomenon). Stories can involve both kinds of conflict. First, look for the conflicts in this story; then for comparison, recall conflicts from other stories you've read.

	Thunder Rolling in the Mountains	**From Other Reading**
Man Against Man		
Man Against Nature		
Group Against Group		
Internal— Man Against Himself		

Evaluating your Solutions to a Problem

Directions: State the problem in a short sentence or two.

_____

_____

In the boxes, answer the evaluation questions for each solution idea.

Problem	Criterion #1 for evaluation: Does it break any laws?	Criterion #2 for evaluation: Is it efficient?	Criterion #3 for evaluation: Is it harmful to anyone?
Solution #1			
Solution #2			
Solution #3			
Solution #4			
Solution #5			

Chapter One

While gathering roots, Sound of Running Feet and her cousins talk to Jason Upright, a white settler.

Vocabulary

travois   cous   scraggly   hillock
kouse

Discussion Questions

1. Who tells the story? (*Sound of Running Feet, a fourteen-year-old female Nez Perce*)

2. How does the author get you into the story? (*written in first person, starts with some action, introducing the characters and their situation through the eyes of the female storyteller*)

3. How do the people in the story tell time? Cite examples from the book. (*by natural phenomenon, "three suns"*) Compare to how you tell time.

4. How does Sound of Running Feet feel about the white settlers? (*angry, unhappy, resentful*) How do you know? (*direct statements, action—shooting at the settler's pan*)

5. How does Jason Upright feel about the Indians? (*angry; He thinks he has a right to settle [and take over] the Indian lands.*)

Chapter Two

Sound of Running Feet reports to her father about the white settlers. General Howard confronts Chief Joseph. Reader meets the Red Coats and Swan Necklace.

Vocabulary

devour   rovers   thrashing   realm
sprawling   banish

Discussion Questions

1. Who is Sound of Running Feet's father? (*Joseph, chieftain of the Ne-mee-poo*)

2. Why does General Howard talk to Chief Joseph? (*He is asking why the Indians aren't preparing to move.*)

3. Who are the Red Coats? (*Indian warriors who have sworn to fight General Howard and his soldiers to their death: Wah-lit-its, Red Moccasin Tops, and Swan Necklace, who guards their horses.*)

4. How does Swan Necklace come to have the horse guarding duty? (*His father is unhappy that Swan Necklace was collecting materials to paint when the Indians were surrounded by soldiers.*)

5. Are the Red Coats justified in their attitudes? How will the Red Coats figure in the story? Make predictions.

Supplementary Activities

1. Art of the Novel: Similes—Explain these similes from Chapters One and Two: "quiet as mice when an owl is around" (page 3), and "flapped like birds ready to fly away" (page 7). What is a simile? Why are similes helpful in books? When do you use similes?

2. Conflict in the Novel: Look for conflicts in the story (see page 14 of this guide).

   Man against Man
   Man against Nature
   Group against Group

3. Collect a list of the names in the book. How are the names like and unlike names you use yourself?

4. How do authors start books? Make a class list of the most intriguing beginnings of books. Then either write a short paragraph to summarize your information on beginnings or write the first two paragraphs for a book you might write.

5. What do you expect of a book narrated by a young Indian girl? Discuss with a partner.

Chapter Three

General Howard and Chief Joseph talk. Joseph agrees to move. There's unrest among the Indians.

Vocabulary

torrents   glint

Discussion Questions

1. Why does Chief Joseph (Thunder Rolling in the Mountains) want to stay with his followers in Wallowa? *(He had received his name from his guardian spirit after 5 days on the mountain overlooking the area. He'd also looked at the proposed new area and thought it wouldn't support the animals.)*

2. Who is Too-hul-hul-sote? *(a large Indian who stands up to General Howard)*

3. Why does Chief Joseph agree to move? *(Answers will vary—law-abiding, force of the military, increasing conflicts with white settlers in their land)*

4. What does Sound of Running Feet think will happen? *(The young warriors won't listen to her father and won't move. Fighting will follow.)*

Chapter Four

Chief Joseph discusses the move and the group is resigned to the action. Swan Necklace and Sound of Running Feet have to postpone their marriage.

Vocabulary

scavengers

Discussion Questions

1. What is the result of the council meeting? *(Chief Joseph will lead the Indians to the new lands in ten days. Some of the group are not entirely supportive.)*

2. Why does Sound of Running Feet give away her rifle? *(She gives it to Swan Necklace, her betrothed, because he needs a weapon.)*

3. What does it mean to "swallow their tears" on page 20? *(The Indians are unhappy about moving but are reluctantly resigned.)*

Supplementary Activities

1. Start attribute webs for Chief Joseph and Sound of Running Feet.

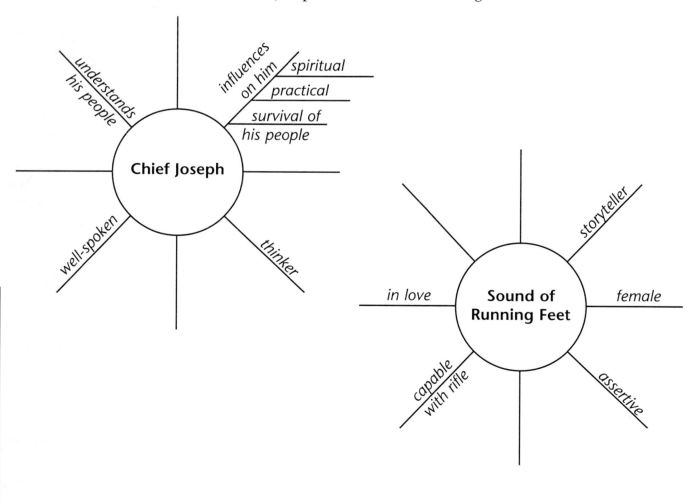

2. Write about what is needed to communicate well. What are barriers to communication? Use examples from the book.

3. If you were told to move as Chief Joseph told his people on pages 18-19, how would you feel?

4. Create an illustration of Chief Joseph and General Howard discussing whether the Indians will move.

Chapter Five

Chief Joseph and other bands of the Nez Perce cross the river to relocate in the new lands, as directed by the general. Chief Joseph's wife, Springtime, tarries and delivers her baby before crossing the river.

Vocabulary

ravine	bullboats	breechcloths	stallion
stampeded	warily	lashed	cradleboards

Discussion Questions

1. What are the dangers in relocating for the Indians? *(The river to be crossed is very deep, swollen with water from the melted snow; temporary shelter on the trail; and finding food)*

2. How do Chief Joseph's people prepare to cross the river? *(They construct rafts and bullboats to take their chosen possessions. They drive the horses and cattle into the river.)*

3. How do the soldiers react to the river crossing? *(They watch from the hill and do not offer to help when rafts are lost.)*

4. Why does Springtime not cross the river with the others? *(She wants her baby to be born in Wallowa, which she considers her home.)*

Chapter Six

The Indians nearly reach the new lands when two white settlers are killed. War with the army is expected.

Vocabulary

kouse mush	ferocious	bootlegger	scalped
flinch	carbine		

Discussion Questions

1. How is it that Swan Necklace reports that Wah-lit-its starts a war? *(Swan Necklace watched when Wah-lit-its, goaded on by insults of his bravery, shoots one of the white settlers. Then another settler is killed.)*

2. How do the various leaders and warriors react to the prospect of war? *(Swan Necklace is exhilarated. Two Moons says it's time to fight. Ferocious Bear says not to go to Lapwai and to kill the soldiers. Chief Joseph wants to make some kind of peace with the army.)*

3. Reread the last sentence of the chapter. What will happen next?

Supplementary Activities

1. Draw a picture of the scene crossing the Snake River.

2. How would you react if you were Chief Joseph at the end of Chapter Six? Discuss with a partner and then write a short paragraph answer.

3. Why does Sound of Running Feet give the extra bullets to Swan Necklace? Would you have acted the same way? Why?

Chapter Seven

The Indians regroup and decide to move to the land over the mountains, planning to live peaceably with the Crows who live there. Sound of Running Feet is in the midst of a battle when she retrieves Red Owl who wanders off.

Vocabulary

clan   butte   pranks

Discussion Questions

1. What does a white flag mean? *(truce to talk)* How do the soldiers react to the Indians' white flag? *(They fire on the party with the white flag.)*

2. The book's narrator says that her father always thinks of the clan first. How is this statement demonstrated in the book? *(He seeks peace which would protect his people. On page 37, he counsels hiding and slipping away because of the size of the force of soldiers. He doesn't want to fight but offers to look after the women, children, and old men.)*

3. How does Sound of Running Feet find herself in a battle? Sort out the events in a flow chart.

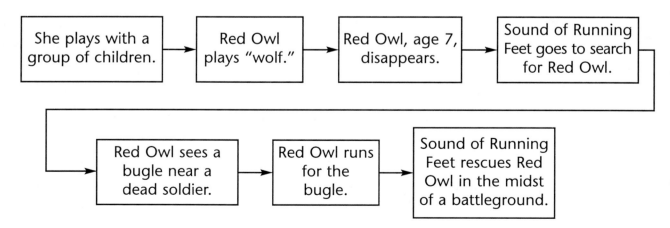

4. How do the Indian warriors feel after the battle? *(exhilarated, successful, rearmed with bullets and rifles taken from dead soldiers, protected and kept safe by their guardian spirits)*

Chapter Eight

The Indians manage to get around the soldiers' barricade as they move toward the land over the mountains.

Vocabulary

barricade

Discussion Questions

1. What kind of obstacles do the Indians encounter as they move on?

Physical	**Human**
rain	Blue Coats
mountains	Indian warriors wanting to fight
boulders on the trail	
animals and possessions they carry	

2. How do the Indians react when they talk to the Montana soldiers? *(They don't want fighting but they don't want to give up their rifles. They decide to slip away in the night.)*

3. The narrator on page 46 says the war is over. Do you agree? What will occur in the rest of the book?

Supplementary Activities

1. Chief Joseph makes decisions in this story. Fill in the decision-making chart to test out alternatives. (See page 15 of this guide.)

2. Look at the map at the start of the book. Plot out the story so far.

3. Review the characters by filling in this chart.

Name	One-word description	Predict importance in the book	Similar to someone I know?
Sound of Running Feet			
Red Owl			
Chief Joseph			
Swan Necklace			
Red Coats			
Blue Coats			

Chapter Nine

The band of Chief Joseph's followers continue their journey. Tales of Coyote, the Indian trickster, are told.

Vocabulary

replenish   trickster   ferocious   scruff

Discussion Questions

1. How do the Indians get needed supplies for their journey? *(They trade horses and gold dust with settlers and traders along the way.)*

2. How does Chief Joseph feel as he leads his people? *(uncertain, sad, apprehensive, resigned)* List each of your answers and then find evidence from the book to support each notion.

3. Who was Coyote? *(an imaginary Indian trickster who had magic powers)* How did Coyote create the many Indian tribes and the large rocks above the Clearwater? *(In a battle with a monster, Coyote cut the monster into pieces. Each piece became a tribe. In an argument with Black Bear, Coyote caught Black Bear in a fishnet and flung him to the other side of the river and turned him to stone.)*

Chapter Ten

The Indian band stops at a pleasant spot for three suns. Although some have foreboding, all seems good until they are attacked in the night by soldiers. Thirty-one Indians are killed and 26 are badly injured.

Vocabulary

taunting   camas roots   tethered   lurched
valiantly   smoldering

Discussion Questions

1. Why do the Indians decide to stay in one place for three suns? *(One of the leaders directs it.)* Is it a wise decision? *(probably not because they are attacked by soldiers)*

2. What is the situation at the end of the chapter? *(Fighting with soldiers has subsided at night but 31 Indians are dead and 26 are badly wounded.)*

3. "Will this hatred ever end?" (page 57) Answer Chief Joseph's query—for the book, and for the present time.

Supplementary Activities

1. Identify and explain these ideas from the book:

   - "The white settlers are like the sands of the river" (page 48).
   - click-clack (page 49)
   - Coyote (page 49)
   - fighting valiantly (page 57)

2. How does the author use sounds to make the story more real? Reread the sound description on page 54 prior to the renewed fighting.

3. Reread Chief Joseph's plea at the end of Chapter Ten, after his wife dies. Survey some adults to gather their reactions. Discuss with classmates and then write a reaction paragraph.

Chapter Eleven

The Indians bury their dead and then move on while the warriors distract the soldiers. Swan Necklace explains the deaths of the other Red Coats.

Vocabulary
travois

Discussion Questions

1. What is the scene at the start of Chapter Eleven? *(The Indians prepare to move on, burying their dead as well as possible first, and then managing to transport the injured.)* How does the author make the scene vivid? *(Answers will vary—details, narrator burying her mother)*

2. Why is this business "a shameful way to fight"? *(Page 60, Women and children are killed by the Blue Coats.)*

3. What does Swan Necklace think protects him? *(his war whistle)* How does Swan Necklace explain the deaths of the other Red Coats? *(He explains that Red Moccasin Tops was shot in the throat while his guardian spirit only protected him from wounds on his body. Wah-lit-its was shot before he could pick up his charm and Rainbow's guardian spirit worked only after sunrise and he was struck at night.)* Some would consider Swan Necklace foolish and superstitious. How do you react?

4. Who is Lean Elk and why is he introduced at the end of Chapter Eleven? *(Page 62, He is a young warrior with a "tight mouth and burning eyes," who is elected as the new leader.)*

Chapter Twelve

The sorry band of Indians moves along, burying dead along the way. When soldiers are spotted nearby, a night raid to disperse their horses and mules and burn their wagons is a success.

Vocabulary
stampeding

Discussion Questions

1. At the start of Chapter Twelve, what is the mood among the band of fleeing Indians? *(grim, angry, resentful of soldiers and of all whites, justified in their killing)* Is this attitude justified? Why or why not?

2. What is the Indian plan to evade the one-armed general and his soldiers? *(capture his horses and mules, and burn his wagons under the cover of darkness)*

3. How does Sound of Running Feet happen to observe the stampeding animals? *(She secretly follows behind the raiding party and is surrounded when the stampeding animals return to the Indian camp.)*

4. How is the Indian mood changed at the end of the chapter? *(They are exhilarated because of beating the soldiers in the raid.)*

Supplementary Activities

1. Collect some of the Indian names on a poster or large bulletin board paper. In short sentences or illustrations, explain the names. Try giving classmates or family members names of the same genre.

2. Is the pursuit of Chief Joseph's Indians fair and right? Is the killing of settlers justified? Discuss with classmates. Try to include various views and sides of the question in your answers.

3. Is Swan Necklace's war whistle like a lucky charm? Explore superstitions and lucky charms in the library.

Chapter Thirteen

Sound of Running Feet is admonished not to play warrior or follow the warriors. Some white settlers are brought to the camp.

Vocabulary

chokecherries   puckered   churning   commotion
skulking

Discussion Questions

1. What is Lean Elk's message and warning to Sound of Running Feet? *(She was definitely in the way on the raid and could have been killed. Lean Elk accused her of costing the Indians a herd of horses.)*

2. What is the Indians' dilemma with the white settlers? *(Chief Joseph doesn't want to harm them but also doesn't want them spying for the soldiers.)*

3. What does Sound of Running Feet learn about white women? *(They act no differently than the Indian women. They calm babies and offer comfort.)*

Chapter Fourteen

Sound of Running Feet observes the white girl. Chief Joseph calls the chieftains into council, and they decide to travel north to join Sitting Bull.

Vocabulary

tethered

Discussion Questions

1. Identify these details from Chapter Fourteen.

	Page	Meaning
Trapped deer	77	The white settler Dirty Face's manner and appearance
Yellow Hair	76	One of the white settlers
click-clack	79	Telegraph by which information about the Indians could be sent
Old Lady's Country	80	Canada
Sitting Bull	80	Indian leader

2. What is the reception of the Crows? *(friendly but unwilling to help lest the white soldiers turn on them also)*

3. How do the Indians evade the soldiers? *(narrow passages through the mountains)*

Supplementary Activities

1. Choose one of the following to describe on a Venn diagram.

   Indian Women / White Women
   Chief Joseph / Ferocious Bear
   Soldiers / Indian Band
   War in the book / War today

2. Try writing in journal style as though you are Sound of Running Feet. What might you have written in Chapters Thirteen and Fourteen?

3. What were the barriers to communication between the Indians and the white settlers, particularly in this book? What might have been done to overcome the barriers?

Chapter Fifteen

The Blue Coats catch up with the Indians in three days. The Crows fight beside the Blue Coats. The Nez Perce continue their journey.

Discussion Questions

1. Why does Swan Necklace use the description "bitter day" (page 82)? *(He speaks in short significant phrases. Though the immediate battle is a success for the Nez Perce, the Crow joining the Blue Coats is a very bad sign. The band under Chief Joseph is low on food.)*

2. Look for sentences or phrases that give you an idea of the rest of the story. *(Answers will vary. Look for clear logical explanations of student choices. Possibilities include: Page 82, "As long as I live no Blue Coat will harm you." Page 83, "Our food ran low." Page 84, "My father's eyes were hard and angry." Page 84, "The white men had fled." Page 85, "...a cold wind")*

Chapter Sixteen

The chiefs disagree about what to do next. Swan Necklace talks of marriage but Sound of Running Feet doesn't feel at peace.

Vocabulary

gullies   misshapen

Discussion Questions

1. What are the different ideas about what the Indians should do? What facts support each idea?

Ideas	Reasons	Proponent
to rest	tired cold no joy in camp	women
to keep going	3 suns from Old Lady's Country Blue Coats on their trail	Lean Elk
to move more slowly	rest people and horses buffalo country can provide food	Looking Glass

2. Why is the narrator worried? *(The retreat is not going well and there is disagreement among the chiefs and warriors.)*

3. How does Swan Necklace's mood differ from the narrator's? *(He is planning for their marriage. He is thinking about the future.)*

Supplementary Activities

1. Plot the emotional tone of each chapter of the book with a single word or a small illustration.

2. Fill in a story map to review the elements of the story. Use either short phrases or sketches.

Chapter Seventeen

The air is cooler when a buffalo stampede announces a renewed fight with the Blue Coats.

Vocabulary

stampede   gulch   bolted   breechcloths

Discussion Questions

1. Choose a title for Chapter Seventeen. Explain your answer. *(Answers will vary but should reflect the plot—stampede, fighting in winter, etc.)*

2. Describe the scene with Swan Necklace and Sound of Running Feet in battle fighting the Blue Coats (page 94).

3. What are buffalo horn cups and how are they used in the book? *(They are cups made from buffalo horns used as water vessels and as digging tools.)*

4. What is the significance of the Cheyenne warrior? *(He is a scout for the Blue Coats. He signifies continued warfare, and lack of solidarity among the Indians.)*

5. How does this battle turn out? *(badly for the Indians—many are dead)*

Chapter Eighteen

Entrenched in positions, the battle continues until the soldiers call a truce. When the talks go badly, Chief Joseph is taken captive. An exchange is later worked out and he's returned. The shooting resumes.

Vocabulary

sharpshooters

Discussion Questions

1. Why are the tunnels built? *(The Indians build tunnels so they can crawl about with less danger of being shot.)*

2. How are the Indians tricked by the truce? *(When Chief Joseph meets Colonel Miles in the space between camps and after talking and disagreeing, Chief Joseph is taken prisoner by the Blue Coats.)*

3. What "strange happening" resolves Chief Joseph's capture? *(A white officer, Lieutenant Jerome, rides into the Indian camp. He is exchanged for Chief Joseph.)*

4. How do you think the Indians feel at the end of Chapter Eighteen? *(betrayed and lied to again by the soldiers)*

5. Why do the authors include the reference on page 97 to Bending Willow's age? *(reminder of how long the Indians have been moving; personal narrator note)*

Supplementary Activities

1. How many ways do the Indians use the buffalo? Do some research in the book and elsewhere. Collect your information on a chart.

2. What does a truce mean? Create a word map.

Word Map for a Noun

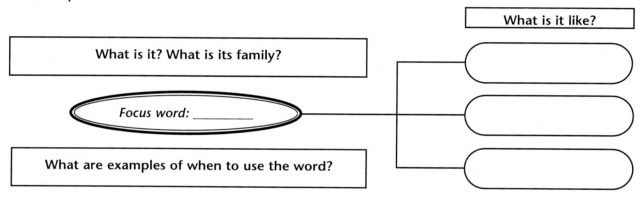

3. Write a short paragraph describing a time you've called a truce.

Chapter Nineteen

The fighting stops. Chief Joseph surrenders to Colonel Miles.

Vocabulary

papoose

Discussion Questions

1. Compare the treatment of Chief Joseph and Lieutenant Jerome when held captive.

Chief Joseph	Lieutenant Jerome
• hands tied behind him and bound to his feet • rolled in a blanket, unable to stand or walk • guarded but also talked to • left to sleep with the mules, without food or water	• slept in a tent • given water and food • provided with a buffalo robe for warmth • was not bound and tied with ropes

2. Why does Chief Joseph surrender? *(He is tired, food is scarce, many have been killed, it is winter, Looking Glass has been killed.)*

3. Why does Sound of Running Feet find herself unable to join the surrendering Indians? *(Answers will vary. She is unable to give up. She is sad.)*

4. Why does Chief Joseph surrender his rifle to Colonel Miles? *(He is the Blue Coat who defeated him. Old enmity exists with General Howard, the one-armed general.)*

Chapter Twenty

Sound of Running Feet, joined by Swan Necklace, heads for Sitting Bull in the Old Lady's country. They meet an Assiniboin hunting party and go with them to their village.

Vocabulary

nickered

Discussion Questions

1. Why does Sound of Running Feet decide to set out alone for the Old Lady's country? *(Others have already left while her father talks to the generals. She decides she cannot surrender to the Blue Coats.)*

2. What is the Old Lady's Country? *(Canada, part of the British holdings under Queen Victoria who reigned from 1837-1901)*

3. Why does Swan Necklace join Sound of Running Feet on her journey? *(He hasn't surrendered with the other warriors and thinks it better that they die together than trust the whites who speak with two tongues.)*

4. Where do the pair head at the end of the chapter? *(They join a hunting party going to their Assiniboin village.)*

5. Why is Sound of Running Feet uncertain and apprehensive en route to the Assiniboin village? *(She isn't trusting. Other Indians have joined the Blue Coats against her people. She sees that these Indians have older guns and that they have noticed the rifles she and Swan Necklace carry.)* How will the book end?

Supplementary Activities

1. Translate each of these expressions into what you'd say today.

   those who speak with two tongues _____

   snows _____

   moons _____

   suns _____

   the star that never moves _____

2. Translate these similes into another expression.

   Page 103, "pain in their eyes" _____

   Page 111, "like a woodpecker pounding on a large pole" _____

   _____

   Page 111, "Its icy fingers poked under our robes and made us shiver." _____

   _____

3. Choose a scene to illustrate:

   Page 106—Chief Joseph and Colonel Miles talking
   Page 107—The long lines of people surrendering to Colonel Miles
   Page 109—Swan Necklace finding Sound of Running Feet
   Page 111—Meeting up with the Assiniboin hunting party

Chapter Twenty-one

Swan Necklace and Sound of Running Feet accompany Red Elk to the Assiniboin village. Swan Necklace is killed and Sound of Running Feet is taken captive.

Vocabulary

tethered   unseemly   noose

Discussion Questions

1. How do Red Elk's people react when they first see Swan Necklace and Sound of Running Feet? (*unrestrained curiosity, staring, feeling their clothes, pointing at them*)

2. Why does Alighting Dove at first seem kind? (*She gives Sound of Running Feet new moccasins.*) Are these first impressions accurate?

3. What is Swan Necklace's fate? (*He is stabbed by Charging Hawk who binds Sound of Running Feet.*)

4. How will the story end? Make a prediction.

Chapter Twenty-two

Charging Hawk means to marry Sound of Running Feet but the girl escapes from her wedding celebration.

Vocabulary
treachery

Discussion Questions
1. What does Sound of Running Feet learn as she begins to understand Assiniboin words? *(Charging Hawk has plans to marry Sound of Running Feet.)*

2. What kind of a person is Charging Hawk? *(ruthless, fierce warrior, excellent marksman with bow and arrow, skillful hunter)*

3. What does Alighting Dove teach Sound of Running Feet? *(Assiniboin way of cooking)*

4. What is the significance of ear piercing? *(When her ears have healed, Sound of Running Feet can marry Charging Hawk.)*

5. How does Sound of Running Feet escape? *(When the dancing is in full swing and it is dark, she takes the ermine blanket, a rifle and bullets, and runs as fast as she can.)*

Supplementary Activities
1. Create a picture of the wedding celebration. Use narrative, sketch, or sound as your medium.

2. Compare the Chapter Twenty-two marriage feast and a wedding you've attended recently. Use a T-chart to collect information and then transfer to a Venn diagram.

Marriage Feast	Wedding You've Attended Recently
whole tribe attends	
parents of groom ask blessings	
pipe smoked by men attending	
dancing	

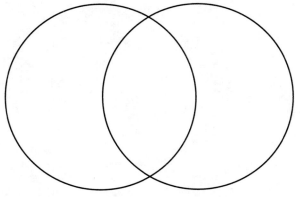

Chapter Twenty-three

Sound of Running Feet escapes from Charging Hawk. She has the chance to shoot him with her rifle but, remembering all the death she's seen, she cannot. Her ordeal is over.

Discussion Questions

1. How is Sound of Running Feet able to escape? *(She pushes herself to run. Resting under the white wedding blanket, she is camouflaged from discovery.)* How is her name well chosen? *(She is able to escape because of her ability to run, as well as her cunning.)*

2. Why doesn't Charging Hawk find Sound of Running Feet? *(He is very tired and her hiding place hides her well.)*

3. Why doesn't Sound of Running Feet shoot Charging Hawk? *(She remembers all the death and decides that some of the killing has to stop.)*

Afterword

Discussion Questions

1. What is an afterword? *(a note included at the end of a book to explain some details of the book, often used with historical novels to give a nonfiction account of how the characters fared)*

2. What is your feeling after reading the afterword? Why?

Concluding Activities

1. Who are the heroes of the book? Why? Complete the Hero identification graphic handout (page 34 of this guide).

2. *Thunder Rolling in the Mountains* is an example of historical fiction. Complete the Historical Fiction Investigation handout (page 35 of this guide).

3. Choose one of these to write about:

   a. Betrayal is a major theme in the book. Cite examples from the book. Finish with a definition.
   b. Chief Joseph is a memorable leader.
   c. Chief Joseph said, "All men were made by the same Great Spirit Chief. Yet we shoot one another down like animals" (page 57). Why do we have warfare?

Heroes

I nominate _____

from *Thunder Rolling in the Mountains* as a hero.

The dictionary defines a hero as _____

_____

My nominee qualifies because _____

_____

Ideas and quotes about heroes: _____

_____

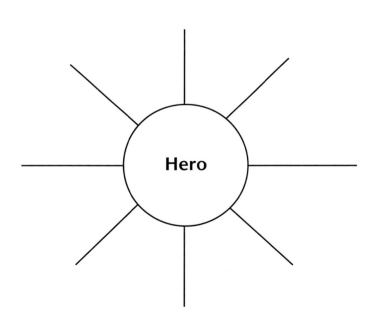

Dictionary definition:

What do you learn from historical fiction? Why is historical fiction a perennial favorite?

Important ideas for me to remember about historical fiction:

Historical Fiction

Challenges in reading historical fiction:

Comparison of historical fiction and other fiction:

Fiction	Historical Fiction

My favorite pieces of historical fiction:

Assessment for *Thunder Rolling in the Mountains*

Assessment is an ongoing process. The following ten items can be completed during the novel study. Once finished, the student and teacher will check the work. Points may be added to indicate the level of understanding.

Name _____ Date _____

Student	**Teacher**	
_____	_____	1. Complete five of the vocabulary activities from page 4 of this guide.
_____	_____	2. Complete a predicting chart as the book is read (pages 8-9 of this guide).
_____	_____	3. Fill in Conflicts in Literature chart on page 14 of this guide.
_____	_____	4. Complete the Hero Identification handout (page 34 of this guide).
_____	_____	5. Explain historical fiction by responding to questions on the Historical Fiction handout (page 35 of this guide).
_____	_____	6. Choose one of the topics from the Concluding Activities on page 33 of this guide for a multi-paragraph piece.
_____	_____	7. Appear as one of the secondary characters in the book. Explain your significance to the class.
_____	_____	8. Choose an event in the book to plot out as a flow chart. (See page 20 of this guide.)
_____	_____	9. Rework one of the comparisons discussed in the novel study, so you could explain it to a parent.
_____	_____	10. Explain in a letter or orally why O'Dell is an important author.